Withdrawn

ANIMATION MAGIC

ANIMATION MAGIC

A BEHIND-THE-SCENES LOOK AT HOW AN ANIMATED FILM IS MADE

DON HAHN

Disney PRESS

New York

✓9/7/97

Printed and bound in the United States of America.
For information address Disney Press,
14 Fifth Avenue, New York, New York 10011–5690.
First Edition
0 9 8 7 6 5 4 3 2 1

Library of Congress Cataloging-in-Publication Data
Hahn, Don.
    Disney's animation magic : a behind-the -scenes look at how an
animated film is made / by Don Hahn—1st ed.
        p.   cm.
    Summary: Discusses the techniques and people involved in creating
Disney's animated films, from the first story idea to opening night.
    ISBN 0-7868-3072-7 (trade)—ISBN 0-7868-5041-8 (lib. bdg.)
    1. Walt Disney Company—Juvenile literature. 2. Animated films—
United States —Juvenile literature. [1. Walt Disney Company.
2. Animated films.] I. Title. II. Title: Animation magic
NC1766.U52D5425 1996
791.43'3—dc20   95-50050

ACKNOWLEDGMENTS
My appreciation and admiration to the hundreds
of gifted Disney animators, artists, and crafts-
people whose work has inspired this book. To Peter
Schneider for his encouragement, and to Eric
Larsen and Walt Stanchfield, who taught me about
animation when I knew nothing. To Katie Alexander,
Patti Conklin, Jon Glick, Cathy Hapka, Ellen
Mendlow, Steve Rogers, Charles Solomon, Lella
Smith, and Larry Ishino, as well as the crew of The
Animation Research Library and The Disney
Archives. Special thanks to Howard Reeves for his
guidance. Thanks, finally, to Randy and Margaret
for everything, and to Denise and Emilie, who
stayed up and waited for me on those late nights
when I was out making cartoons.

Design produced by Welcome Enterprises, Inc.
Design by Mary Tiegreen.
Photography by Michael Stern.

Page 1: A cleanup drawing of Lumiere with markup
instructions for ink and paint.
Pages 2–3: Aladdin's Genie.
Pages 4–5: A dynamic background painting of the
Cathedral of Notre Dame from The Hunchback of
Notre Dame and a rough animation drawing from
The Ugly Duckling (inset).
Pages 6–7: John Smith in Pocahontas

To Emilie

CONTENTS

PROLOGUE

HOW'D THEY DO THAT?

I remember the first time I went to the theater to see a Disney animated film. I was so young that it never occurred to me that Mowgli and Baloo were anything but real—totally real. It was magic! ■ One day my best friend told me that people actually sat down and drew these films. My illusions were shattered—like someone saying, "There's no Santa Claus!" He said animated movies were actually done by people who started with a blank piece of paper and drew everything you see on the screen. I thought, "Imagine getting paid for goin' to work and drawing cartoons all day long. That's for me!" ■ Nowhere is there more magic, wonder, and illusion than in a Disney animated film. From start to finish, the making of an animated film is an amazing process. Six hundred people work for four years to create a million drawings that will be projected at twenty-four frames per second, and if everyone does their job, you will laugh, be moved to tears . . . and be transported to a different world. ■ If you've ever seen a Disney animated feature and wondered, "How'd they do that?" then this book is for you. It's your private guided tour "backstage" at the Disney animation studios to see how the artists start with a blank piece of paper and create the many wonders of Disney character animation.

ACT 1
THE IDEA

I'VE GOT AN IDEA

Walt Disney was an artist and storyteller who became fascinated with animation when he was a young cartoonist in Kansas City, Missouri. To him, animation was a story-

telling medium that had no limits. His nephew Roy Disney once said that there are three things that make a Disney animated film so special: "story, story, and story." ■ A good movie starts with a good idea for a good story. Some stories—Beauty and the Beast, Snow White and the Seven Dwarfs—come from fairy tales. Or a film might be adapted from a book like *The Hunchback of Notre Dame, Bambi,* or *The Jungle Book.* And in some films, like *The Lion King,* the story grows out of an original idea. ■ A small team of writers and artists begin exploring the story's potential in much the same way a journalist might investigate a newspaper story. These development artists explore in both words and drawings the who, what, when, where, why, and how of the story. They also explore the "wow" of the story. That's the extra factor that makes a story just perfect for animation. It's hard to imagine Aladdin's genie, Alice's wonderland, or a flying elephant named Dumbo

Pages 8–9: Ideas come in all shapes and sizes—like the pre-production painting for The Hunchback of Notre Dame *or the quick sketch of the cast of* The Jungle Book.

A delicate pastel sketch of Bambi (left). Walt Disney at his animation desk (below).

Opposite: Preproduction drawings must capture an emotion quickly in one sketch, like those from "The Sorcerer's Apprentice," The Jungle Book, The Hunchback of Notre Dame, The Great Mouse Detective, *or* The Sword in the Stone *(clockwise from upper left).*

appearing in a live-action movie. That's because they're all things that best come to life in animation. ■ Good stories also have a good clear theme, like "don't judge a book by its cover" in *Beauty and the Beast*. All of the characters—Belle, the Beast, Gaston, the objects—are one thing on the outside and something completely different on the inside. The Beast is the ugly monster with the heart of gold, Gaston is handsome but with the heart of a monster. ■ Along with theme, good stories also have at their core a very basic action. For example, you could describe the central action of *The Lion King* as "go home." Here are some more examples:

The Little Mermaid and *Cinderella*
"GET THE PRINCE"

Rescuers Down Under
"FIND THE BOY"

The Hunchback of Notre Dame
"GET OUT THERE"

101 Dalmatians
"FIND THE PUPPIES"

Snow White and the Seven Dwarfs
"STOP THE WICKED QUEEN"

Beauty and the Beast
"BREAK THE SPELL"

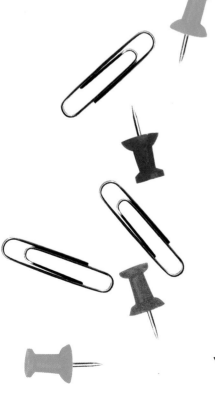

Go, Team

Animation is a team sport. Yes, there are leaders and followers, but for the most part, an animated film is created by a team of very creative people.

The **PRODUCER** is the team builder, coach, and cheerleader all wrapped into one. In addition to taking care of budgets, schedules, and contracts, a producer also has an important creative role in helping the directors tell their story. The producer and directors are the leaders of the film. You'll see them show up a lot as we follow the process of making an animated movie.

The **DIRECTORS** are the chief storytellers—the creative leaders of a film. They must guide the writers, actors, animators, and musicians toward the same goal—and ensure that they all tell the same story. Making an animated film is so complex and time consuming that there are usually two directors who work together to direct a film. The codirectors form a close partnership and share equally in the tasks and decisions. Rob Minkoff, codirector of *The Lion King*, says the process of directing an animated film is like conducting a symphony orchestra one instrument at a time. Just like a member of an orchestra, each artist works independently toward a common goal. And the results are often greater than any one individual could achieve.

Early idea sketches for Aladdin (below) and The Lion King (opposite below right) done years before those movies were finished. (Opposite left) Lyricist Stephen Schwartz (standing) and composer Alan Menken (seated) listen to "Out There" at a recording session. A finished storyboard (opposite right) looks like a giant comic book.

WRITERS join a project early to write a script. The script doesn't just supply the dialogue that the characters will say—it also describes the people, places, and forces at work in the story. Animation is a visual medium, so the writers work closely with the story artists to create characters and situations that will work well visually.

A **STORY ARTIST** is a unique person who can both draw and tell a story. Early on in the development of a film, story artists might draw gags or bits of action that indicate character action, staging, or emotion. Later they will begin to sketch out entire sequences of the film and then pin their story sketches to a storyboard so the sequence can be discussed in a story meeting. All the while, the story artist is looking for ideas that will further develop the characters and the plot.

SONGWRITERS

usually work collaboratively—one person writes the lyrics, and another writes the music. Songs are important because they express the major turning points in the story. In the development of an animated film, the songwriters are an essential part of the storytelling team. Imagine *The Little Mermaid* without "Under the Sea" or *The Jungle Book* without "Bare Necessities." The songs become some of the most memorable moments in the film. In Walt Disney's day, songs were so critical to the animation process that they called the director's office the Music Room. It was the place where the producer, director, writer, musician, and story artist would work out the details of the film bit by bit.

TELL ME ABOUT IT

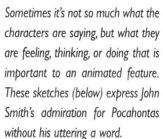

People love to hear stories—bedtime stories, news stories, sports stories, stories about people and places and things in the world around us. Some stories are about very real things and some are complete fantasies. Most often stories are told by one person—an author, a newscaster, a film director. But in animation, perhaps more than in any other medium, everyone who works on the film is a storyteller. ■ On an animated film, the directors provide the vision for the type of story they want to tell. They work closely with the writers, story artists, and songwriters to create a story outline board. This outline usually consists of strips of paper pinned to a storyboard that describe, beat by beat, the plot of the film. Putting the entire film on an outline board keeps the plot clear and simple in everybody's minds. The writers and song-writers will begin writing scenes and songs for the film, always working with the director to find what is most interesting and entertaining about the story. Directors are careful not to have characters say what can be shown. John Smith doesn't need to say, "Gee, Pocahontas, you sure are pretty, standing there in front of that waterfall."

The personalities of Cogsworth and Lumiere first emerged in story sketches (above) that not only show the characters reacting to Belle's arrival at the Beast's castle but also contrast Cogsworth's cautious attitude with Lumiere's open joy.

Sometimes it's not so much what the characters are saying, but what they are feeling, thinking, or doing that is important to an animated feature. These sketches (below) express John Smith's admiration for Pocahontas without his uttering a word.

The climax of The Lion King (right) places Simba and the hyenas high atop Pride Rock as the Pride Lands burn below. Story artists develop dramatic staging ideas that help tell the story.

His facial expressions and actions convey the same sentiment. It's much easier and stronger to show it than to tell it. Some characters, like Dumbo, Dopey, and Abu, never say a word but it's completely clear what

they're thinking. The magic carpet in *Aladdin* doesn't even have a face—yet you know what it's up to. ■ The story artists will take a small section of the script and begin to visualize it sketch by sketch on a storyboard. They'll look for ways to improve the script with new ideas for action or dialogue. In story meetings with

the directors, the storyboards are worked, reworked, and polished until they are a solid bit of storytelling. Lots of ideas develop in this stage and lots of ideas are thrown out, too. ■ Some storyboards, like the wildebeest stampede in *The Lion King*, have very little dialogue and are based on action. Other sequences are based on fast-talking humor—just think of Pumbaa and Timon—or on sensitive dialogue, as when Belle confesses her love to the dying Beast. ■ Storyboarding does not always start from the beginning of a film. In *The Lion King*, one of the first storyboards completed was the Mufasa's ghost sequence. Even though this moment occurs in the middle of the movie, it told the film-

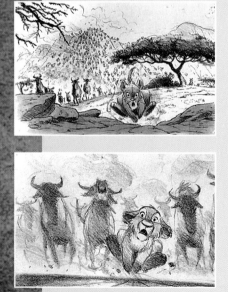

makers a lot about the character of Simba and his relationship with his father and Rafiki. The sequence became the core of the film and everything grew out of it. ■ Songs are often written and storyboarded early in the process because they provide the story "tent poles" for the whole movie. That's because in a musical, songs usually occur at critical turning points. If the songs are in the right places, they will provide good support for the rest of the story. Songwriters try to avoid "sitting duck" songs, which stop the story completely while the characters sing. No audience wants to sit through a song about something they don't care about.

These story sketches of the Beast's magical transformation (left) or of Mufasa's awesome ghost (below and opposite) not only told the story, but they also suggested how these moments might appear in the final film.

You can almost feel the ground shaking in these two story sketches (left) of Simba running for his life.

These story sketches of Pumbaa and Timon (opposite) are very simple and cartoonlike, but they communicate Timon's joke quickly and clearly.

Hakuna matata!

Hakuna matata?

Yeah, it's our motto.

What's a motto?

Nothin'. What's a motto with you?

Laff

DON'T I KNOW YOU?

We need characters to tell a story. Character ideas spring from people around us in everyday life. Friends, moms, aunts and uncles, bosses, enemies, the kid next door—they all have the stuff from which good characters are made. Aladdin codirector Ron Clements says, "The more you know someone the more you care about them, and the more you care about them, the more you will take interest in their story . . . in the outcome of their life."

HEROES

Many of the oldest and most revered stories track the journey of a heroic character. *The Odyssey, Star Wars,* and *The Lion King* are all "hero's journey" stories. A hero or heroine leaves home, encounters many obstacles, seeks advice from a wise person, and finally returns home to conquer his or her worst enemy.

COMPANIONS

Every hero has traveling companions. Our hero sometimes just needs someone to talk to. When times get tough, Ariel can turn to Flounder. Pocahontas has Meeko and Flit. Quasimodo's companions, the gargoyles, are more than listeners; they take on the role of his conscience, or inner voice. The Beast's objects act as friend, coach, and confidant.

VILLAINS

The villain is the obstacle, the counterpoint to our hero. Some bad guys, like Scar, befriend the hero only to stab him in the back later. Some, like Governor Ratcliffe or Cruella de Vil, are more direct about what they want. Some, like Gaston, may seem foolish on the surface, but turn out to be very real threats to our hero.

FOOLS

Sidekicks sometimes move the plot forward, but most often provide fun, gags, and entertainment value. Sidekicks like Lefou (French for "the fool"), Smee, Scuttle, and Ed the hyena are all just along for the laughs.

PARENTS

Have you ever noticed how many heroes come from nontraditional families? Belle, Jasmine, Pocahontas, and Ariel have no mother. Snow White, Dumbo, and Cinderella have no father. Aurora in *Sleeping Beauty* is separated from her parents. Mowgli, Aladdin, Quasimodo, and the Beast have no parents at all. Part of the subtext of a fairy tale is the journey from childhood and being dependent on parents to adulthood and relying on yourself. ■ Nowhere is this more clearly illustrated than in *The Lion King*, a rare film in which our hero has both a mother and a father. But his life changes abruptly when his father is killed in a stampede. It is that event that marks the beginning of Simba's journey into adulthood.

MENTORS

Rafiki may seem like a crazy old baboon, but if you listen closely, his words are full of wisdom. In most fairy tales there is a "wise old something," like Grandmother Willow, that imparts wisdom to our hero . . . if he or she is willing to listen. In times past, the elder, the grandparent, or the old medicine man was often the most revered person in their community. Why? They were the storytellers who passed on their wisdom and experience from generation to generation.

THE CHORUS

Whether it's a school of fish, talking pots and pans, or an angry mob in Paris, the community plays a part in observing and commenting on the progress of our story. Since the time of the earliest Greek dramas 2,500 years ago, the "chorus" has played a very important role in the story.

Sing Me a Story

The best songs in animation tell the story better than spoken words can. In fact, songs provide a very concentrated way of telling a story. Think of "Hakuna Matata," where years go by as Pumbaa and Timon teach Simba all about their philosophy, and we watch Simba grow from a cub into a full-grown lion. ■ Or consider the opening of *The Hunchback of Notre Dame*, which introduces you to Paris, Clopin, the gypsies, Frollo, Quasimodo's mother, Notre Dame, and the archdeacon and tells the story of how Quasimodo ended up in the bell tower of the church—all in a five-and-a-half-minute song. If you tried to explain all of this in dialogue, the audience would fall asleep. But the song "Bells of Notre Dame" gets the information across in a very entertaining and exciting way. ■ Each song in a musical serves a very specific purpose.

"COLORS OF THE WIND"

THE ANTHEM

An anthem is a song of celebration and hope that states the theme of a film. "Colors of the Wind" became an anthem for Pocahontas. She sings about her reverence for the earth and the harmony between people and nature. Some songs, like Elton John and Tim Rice's "Circle of Life," create an epic atmosphere. "When You Wish upon a Star" quietly expresses Pinocchio's hopes and dreams.

"CAN YOU FEEL THE LOVE TONIGHT?"

THE LOVE SONG

Romance can be expressed beautifully in music. Simba and Nala rekindle their friendship and fall in love during "Can You Feel the Love Tonight." A love song doesn't have to be syrupy sweet, either. In *Lady and the Tramp*, Tramp takes his girl to his favorite Italian restaurant for some leftovers. But instead he gets the specialty of the house—spaghetti—complete with Tony's accordion accompaniment and the song "Bella Notte."

THE "I WANT" SONG

Every hero is on a quest for something in his life. In a musical, that quest is best expressed in a song that some songwriters call the "I want" song. Quasimodo wants nothing more than to "live one day out there." Ariel sings of her longing to be "part of your world." Belle wants "adventure in the great wide some- where."

THE VILLAIN'S SONG

Most bad guys have an evil plot against our hero, and what better way to reveal that plot than in a song like "Be Prepared," "Mine, Mine, Mine," or "Gaston."

"GASTON! GASTON!"

"YOU AIN'T NEVER HAD A FRIEND LIKE ME!"

PURE ENTERTAINMENT

"Be Our Guest," "Under the Sea," and "A Friend Like Me" all carry a bit of the story, but also allow the animator to break out and do what animation does best . . . entertain.

TALK TO ME

After the filmmakers have chosen a story and developed characters to tell that story, the search begins for the voices that will bring those characters to life. Some selections are obvious. It's hard to imagine Mrs. Potts without Angela Lansbury's voice or the Genie without Robin Williams's. But most casting decisions begin with the producer and directors listening to voice tapes of dozens of actors until they find the perfect voice. ■ Try this as an experiment. Tune in to a sitcom on TV. Now turn away from the picture and listen carefully. Some voices are unique and recognizable whenever they speak, while other voices may blend into the crowd or sound ordinary. ■ Now listen to an animated film in the same way. If you listen to the whole cast, the range of voices can be quite different. Like opera singers, some voices are in a high soprano or tenor range (usually the hero or heroine) while others are low and resonant (usually the villain or sometimes a father or old man). This range of casting is important and gives variety to the characters.

The vocal performance of Jeremy Irons influenced the look and feel of Scar (left). Codirectors Kirk Wise and Gary Trousdale discuss a scene with actor Kevin Kline, the voice of Phoebus, at a recording session for The Hunchback of Notre Dame (opposite).

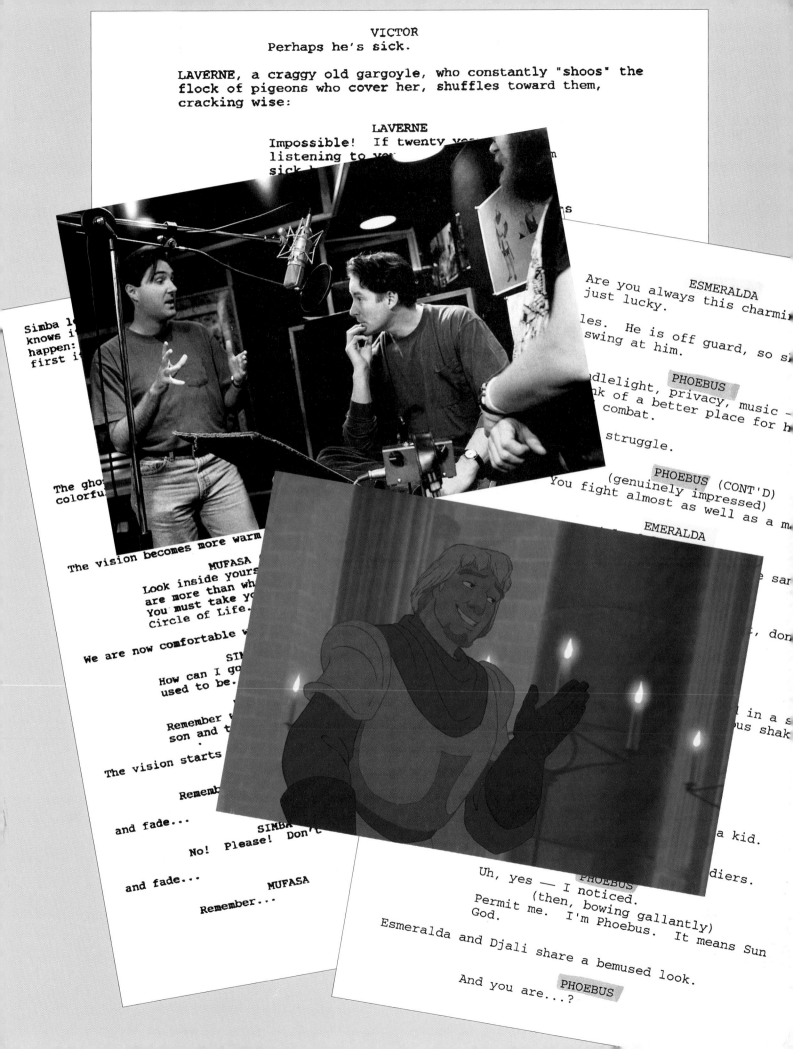

VICTOR
Perhaps he's sick.

LAVERNE, a craggy old gargoyle, who constantly "shoos" the
flock of pigeons who cover her, shuffles toward them,
cracking wise:

LAVERNE
Impossible! If twenty ye...
listening to yo...
sick b...

Simba l...
knows i...
happen:...
first i...

The gho...
colorfu...

The vision becomes more warm...

MUFASA
Look inside yours...
are more than wh...
You must take yo...
Circle of Life.

We are now comfortable w...

SIM...
How can I go...
used to be.

Remember t...
son and t...

The vision starts...

Remembe...

and fade...

SIMB...
No! Please! Don't...

and fade...

MUFASA

Remember...

ESMERALDA
Are you always this charmin...
just lucky.

...les. He is off guard, so s...
swing at him.

PHOEBUS
...dlelight, privacy, music —
...k of a better place for h...
combat.

...struggle.

PHOEBUS (CONT'D)
(genuinely impressed)
You fight almost as well as a m...

EMERALDA

...e sar...

..., don...

...l in a s...
...us shak...

...a kid.

...diers.

PHOEBUS
Uh, yes — I noticed.
(then, bowing gallantly)
Permit me. I'm Phoebus. It means Sun
God.

Esmeralda and Djali share a bemused look.

And you are...? PHOEBUS

BANZAI- NOW THAT'S POWER.

SHENZI- TELL ME ABOUT IT. I JUST HEAR THAT NAME, I SHUDDER. 29.7"

29.7"

BANZAI- "MUFASA"

29.8"

SHENZI- "BBBRRRR!" 29.11"

29.11"

SHENZI- DO IT AGAIN.

The relationship between two voices is very important. For this scene (above) actors Whoopi Goldberg and Cheech Marin needed good comic timing to make the humor of Shenzi and Banzai pay off.

■ The tempo of the voice is important, too. Jafar's slow, calculating delivery contrasts well with Iago's fast-talking comedic voice. Tempo also reveals how a character's mind works. Mufasa's low, resonant voice, calm and always in control, contrasts with the fussy tone of Zazu's quicker tempo of speech. ■ Some characters are better with no voice at all. Think of Meeko and Flit, Dumbo, Dopey, Abu, and Djali the goat. These characters are just as entertaining without speaking a word. Their expressions and actions tell the audience every-thing. ■ Once the voice actors are selected, they come in and record their lines of dialogue. The voice actors are always recorded *before* any animation drawings are done, since their delivery, timing, and attitude will inspire the animation that follows. ■ A voice actor usually comes in to record five or six times over a period of a year. With each session, new sections of the movie are recorded along with rewritten bits of dialogue from previous recording sessions. The actors are seldom recorded together in the same place, so the directors often edit together a "radio show" of all the actors' performances to hear how the dialogue is playing and how the voices interact. ■ Then the radio show is put together with filmed story sketches to see if voice and sketch combine to tell the story. This is called the story reel, or work reel, and it allows the filmmakers to sit down and evaluate how the entire film is shaping up from start to finish.

Dopey (above) is one of Disney's most beloved characters, yet he never utters a sound. His facial expressions and actions convey his thoughts and emotions.

ANGELA LANSBURY DELIVERS TEA AND SYMPATHY AS MRS. POTTS. LINDA LARKIN IS THE SPEAKING VOICE OF PRINCESS JASMINE. LEA SALONGA (NOT PICTURED) SANG THE PART. IF AN ACTOR CAN'T SING, ANOTHER ACTOR

PROVIDES THE SINGING VOICE. JODI BENSON PROVIDED BOTH THE SPEAKING VOICE AND SINGING VOICE FOR ARIEL, AS DID ROBBY BENSON FOR THE BEAST. ROBERT GUILLAUME PLAYS SIMBA'S MENTOR, RAFIKI.

SOMETIMES THE PHYSICAL TRAITS OF THE ACTOR BEGIN TO APPEAR IN THE CHARACTER: DAVID OGDEN STIERS AS COGSWORTH; JONATHAN FREEMAN AS JAFAR; AND PAT CARROLL AS URSULA.

A Whole New World

The **ART DIRECTOR** is responsible for the way a movie looks. Everything that you see on the screen has been thought about, debated, and designed with the guidance of the art director. ■ The art director's ultimate task is to create a whole new world on the screen—a world that will interest the audience and help tell the story, too. ■ In *Aladdin*, the art director used color and shape in a very deliberate way to tell

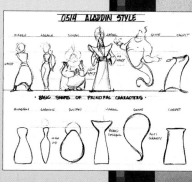

the story. The villains were designed with sharp angles and almost always appeared against hot red backgrounds. The heroes were designed with more pleasing rounded angles and appeared in cool reassuring blue and gold backgrounds. ■ The world created for *The Lion King* was inspired by a real place, Africa.

THE LION KING

But to create a sweeping epic landscape for the film, art director Andy Gaskill made color and lighting choices that actually heighten the reality of each scene. You can almost taste the dust and smell the air and feel the warmth of the African sun. The art direction can help the audience feel as though they have really been to Africa. In *Pocahontas*, Michael Giaimo chose a more

POCAHONTAS

THE HUNCHBACK OF
NOTRE DAME

REMAINS OF
DUNGEON PATCHED UP
WITH STICKS / DEBRIS

PIT

Art directors use paints, pencils, pastels, and markers to create hundreds of pieces of art to try to find the right look for a movie. These pieces from The Rescuers Down Under (above) and Aladdin didn't end up in the movies but still inspired the feelings of those films.

HEY!
WHAT IF THEY
ACTUALLY LIVE
IN THE POTS?
(-A SORT OF
JUNKYARD OF
POTTERY.)

WITH THE
MONKEYS?

stylized approach for design and color. Strong verticals and horizontals, and an overall simplicity of characters and background, help the audience appreciate the elegance of *Pocahontas*'s beautiful natural environment. ■ Remember that in animation, everyone is a storyteller. The art director can use color and shape and design to make you feel a certain way about a character or a place. Dave

Goetz knew that *The Hunchback of Notre Dame* was a story about contrasts—the haves vs. the have-nots. So he built contrasts into the backgrounds: sunlight vs. shadow, warm colors vs. cool colors, bright colors vs. dark, moody colors. ■ We all have feelings when it comes to

color. A clear blue sky, a foggy gray morning, and a blazing red sunset each makes us feel a certain way. The colors chosen for characters and their settings also tell us about who they are. ■ This visual storytelling is something animation can do better than any live-action film. In live action, the art director is usually limited by what can be built and filmed in the real world with real people. In animation, the art director can create a world that you can only dream of. Sometimes, the worlds of live action and animation can collide, and the result becomes its own reality. *Mary Poppins* put people in a fantasy world and *Who Framed Roger Rabbit* put Toons in the real world.

Good art direction supports the story and the characters. Skull Rock (opposite) is the perfect backdrop for the pirates in Peter Pan. Quasimodo's crude tabletop carving of Paris (above) illustrates his loneliness and desire to be a part of the real world in the streets down below him.

Art directors explore not only the setting but also the characters. Quick rough paintings from 101 Dalmatians (top left), Cinderella (top right), and Alice in Wonderland (below left) each have a different style and feeling.

Pages 34–35: Production background of Never Never Land. Cleanup animation drawing of Chernabog from Fantasia's Night on Bald Mountain.

Layouts, like these of the river bend from Pocahontas (opposite), Princess Jasmine's room (top), Gaston's pub (above), and the square in front of the Cathedral of Notre Dame (surrounding), are a reflection of the characters who inhabit them.

ALL THE WORLD'S A STAGE

As the set designers of animation, the **LAYOUT ARTISTS** draw the stage that the animated character will act upon. Their view of the world tells the story, too. ■ At first the layout artist acts as city planner, landscape architect, and interior designer. Streets and buildings, furniture, trees, doors, and windows all must look interesting and

entertaining. But the layout drawing also must be functional for the storytelling of the scene. ■ To make the layouts believable, research is very valuable. Sometimes research means traveling to the land where a story takes place. The crew of *The Lion King* traveled to Kenya to experience the plains and wildlife of Africa. Artists on *The Hunchback of Notre Dame* went to Paris to sketch and photograph the

Cathedral of Notre Dame. ■ Books also help tell the layout artist about the historical accuracy of props and furniture for the era. An animation layout must serve many masters. It is not only functional for the comings and goings of characters, but also gives us a feeling of time, place, scale, character, and mood.

SAY CHEESE

We all love to look at photographs. But a photo offers you only a limited view of the world. For example, take your camera at home and look through the viewfinder. Suddenly the whole world is reduced to what you can see in a small rectangle. The same is true in a movie. The filmmakers show you only a small rectangle of life—so what they show is very important. ■ An animated movie is broken down into large chunks of story, called sequences: the escape sequence, the love sequence, the fight sequence, the happy-ending sequence—you get the idea. Each sequence contains several individual scenes. Each time you cut to a new angle it's called a scene. A typical movie might have twenty sequences and 1,300 scenes. ■ Deciding what the camera should see for each of those scenes is the **LAYOUT ARTIST**'s job. He or she starts by working with the directors on a series of rough drawings that illustrate how every scene in a sequence will look. These drawings determine the camera angle, how the camera moves, the lighting, and

WORKBOOK DRAWINGS DETERMINE THE CAMERA ANGLE, HOW THE CAMERA MOVES, THE LIGHTING, AND THE PATH OF ACTION FOR THE CHARACTER.

This page from The Lion King *layout workbook shows the layout notes for one scene of Simba walking out on a log to look at his reflection. Notice how the camera will move from Simba to the water. Another workbook sketch (opposite top left) calls for the camera to follow Quasimodo as he rescues Esmeralda.*

This workbook drawing from The Lion King (right) has an odd shape because the layout artist needs to draw only what the camera will show as it follows Rafiki from the treetop down to his tortoise shell. Notice how most of the branches and gourds are marked OL (overlay) or UL (underlay). These elements will be drawn on separate pieces of paper and move past the camera at different speeds to create depth.

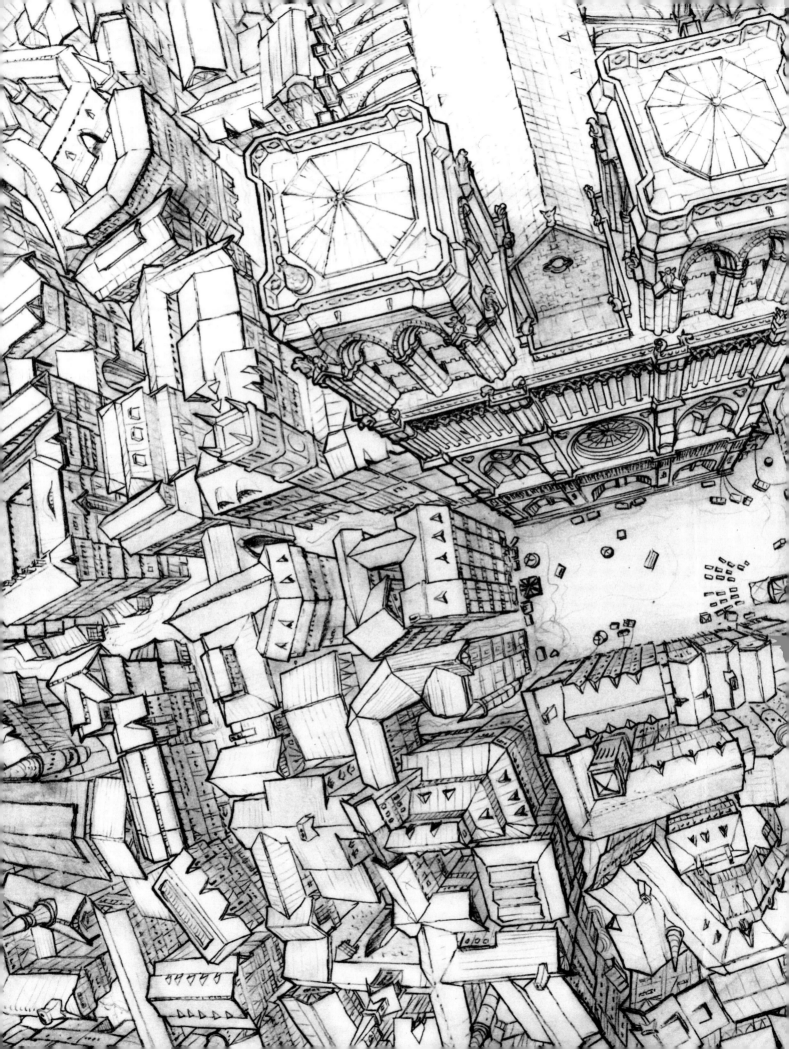

the path of action for the character. The result is a kind of technical version of the storyboard called a workbook. ■ Look through your camera again and then walk toward an object (that's called trucking in) or move from side to side (panning) or rotate your camera so the image is tilted (rotation). All of these moves and more are available to the layout artist to create the feeling of living in and moving through a real world. ■ With the small workbook drawings as a basis, the layout artist creates a large-scale pencil drawing of the setting for each individual scene. The layout is seldom a single drawing of a backdrop. Foreground objects like trees, props, and furniture are drawn on separate pieces of paper so the animated character can move behind them and help create the feeling of space.

Layout artists try to make the audience forget that they are looking at a flat two-dimensional drawing. It almost feels as if you could fall into this layout drawing of Notre Dame (opposite). Miniature models, like this one from Lady and the Tramp (above), help layout artists study perspective and camera angles. In recent years, artists have built similar study models using a computer.

COLOR MY WORLD

Each scene in the movie now has a pencil layout drawing that illustrates the setting for that scene. When that drawing arrives on a background artist's desk, their task is to create a painting based exactly on that layout, but full of color, light, and mood. **BACKGROUND ARTISTS** are storytellers, too. ■ The background artist must keep the audience focused on the character and the story. Where is the character in the background? What time of day is it? At what point does this scene appear in the movie? Is the moment sad or mysterious or celebratory? The painter literally paints the story. ■ The background painters work closely with the art director. Early in the filmmaking process the painters will do several small color sketches of the various key moments in the film. These sketches will provide a color map for the film and ensure that the overall movie isn't too dark or light and doesn't stray toward one color or another. ■ After this planning process, the most important backgrounds—called color keys—from each sequence are painted to set the color tone and style for the movie. Then the background artists will go about the demanding process of creating the 1,300 or so individual paintings that will provide the background for the action of the film. ■ Supervising background artist Lisa Keene says, "You've got to remember that a background is just that . . . a background, a stage to support the characters and not to detract from them. The important thing about the final painting is the emotion of the scene."

Before a background artist can paint a big beautiful painting, like this one from Pocahontas (background), he or she will explore colors and lighting in smaller paintings called color keys. Background supervisor Lisa Keene (above) at work on some color keys for The Hunchback of Notre Dame. Notice the variety of styles in these small color keys from Sleeping Beauty (opposite top), The Hunchback of Notre Dame (opposite, middle and bottom), Pocahontas (right), and Aladdin (below right).

Pages 42–43: Small color key paintings from Aladdin (left) and The Hunchback of Notre Dame (right). Masterful lighting and perspective in this background (background) enhance the dog's-eye view of the world in Lady and the Tramp.

The feeling of a film can be affected by the choice of painting techniques: (right) the transparent watercolors of Pinocchio give the film its story-book quality; (opposite top) the oil paint forest from Bambi is soft and inviting; (opposite bottom) the bold cartoonlike color of Alice in Wonderland is fun and quirky; (right middle) gouaches and acrylic paints create a realistic medieval Paris for The Hunchback of Notre Dame; and the black-line overlay blends with the black lines of the characters to create the highly stylized backgrounds for 101 Dalmatians. It is the color key (bottom right) that inspired the final background (below).

DRESS REHEARSAL

COMIC OR NOBLE?

The story people have worked out a character's role in the story, and the layout and background artists have set the stage, and now we're ready for our "actor" to take the spotlight. Everything about the look, movement, and personality of an animated character is the responsibility of a **SUPERVISING ANIMATOR.** ∎ In animation, the way a character is designed tells us a lot about his or her personality. Without movement or a word of dialogue, a character drawing must convey:

**WHEN THE CHARACTER LIVED
HOW RICH OR POOR THE CHARACTER IS
IF THE CHARACTER IS COMIC OR NOBLE
HOW OLD THE CHARACTER IS
IF WE SHOULD LOVE OR HATE THE CHARACTER
WHAT TIME OF DAY IT IS**

Costumes, hairstyles, and props also inform us about a character's personality. Even animal characters like Scar and Mufasa sport different hairstyles that tell us about who they are. ∎ The supervising animator considers all these factors when designing a character. For example, when Tony Fucile began designing Esmeralda, he gathered story sketches, early development drawings, research on gypsies, and pictures of pretty women. Then, with the inspiration of Demi Moore's vocal performance, the character began to emerge. ∎ Tony collected his favorite drawings and made a "model sheet" so that all the other artists that worked with the character would understand how to draw her. Tony often does some scenes of experimental animation to see how his design works when you start to move it around. This gives him a chance for a dress rehearsal before the directors begin giving him scenes for the movie.

Pinocchio has 3 fingers and thumb

PINOCCHIO'S STANDARD COSTUME -
Feather fastened under band around hat. Hat is not a derby - but is inclined to be peaked. Two suspender buttons on pants in front. Dowl pin thru knee joint. One button on outside of each shoe.

WHAT TIME OF DAY?

RICH OR POOR?

COMIC OR NOBLE?

DO WE LOVE HER OR HATE HER?

WHEN DID HE LIVE?

SEQ 1-1. STANDARD COSTUME WITH APRON DOWN TO BED SHOT WHERE GEPPETTO IS IN NIGHT SHIRT COSTUME.

COMIC OR NOBLE?

HOW OLD IS THIS CHARACTER?

An Actor Prepares

An animator, like any actor, must prepare for the role. Veteran animator Eric Larson, who mentored many of today's Disney animators, said, "One of the last things you should do as an animator is pick up a pencil and start drawing." The thinking and preparation that go into a character are just as important as the drawing itself. ■ On *Beauty and the Beast*, animator Glen Keane asked to get in a cage with a gorilla so he could feel what it was like to be close to such a huge beast. (Lucky for Glen, the zookeeper made him stay outside of the cage to draw.) Animator Andreas Deja went to a gym in Los Angeles to look at the many "Gastons" admiring themselves in the mirror. ■ Animators on *The Lion King* visited countless zoos and wild animal parks and studied miles of nature film footage to help them understand animal locomotion. Then animal expert Jim Fowler brought live lions into the studio. Simba animator Mark Henn said, "The feeling of being a few feet away from a four-hundred-pound lion gave us a new sense of respect for their power and majesty." ■ Another kind of reference is taken from the real world. As human beings, we are very familiar with how the human body acts and moves. So audiences are very unforgiving when it comes to the animation of human charac- ters. Animators often shoot videos of actors in costume to study the move- ment and subtle timing of human characters. ■ Sculptors can help with research, too. As the animator arrives at the final design for the character, sculptures called maquettes are made to help the artists visualize the character from all angles.

A sculptor puts the finishing touches on a maquette of Clopin (above left). Trips to the zoo provide preliminary research for Pumbaa (below left), Simba (below), and the Beast (above).

Real lions model for the animation team (left). A pencil study by Mike Cedeno for Pocahontas (below). Animator Mark Henn sketched the actors during a recording session for The Great Mouse Detective (lower left). Live study models for Anita and Cruella De Vil (lower right) and how the animation eventually captured their action (inset). (Actress Mary Wickes portrays Cruella De Vil here and later provided the voice of Laverne the gargoyle.)

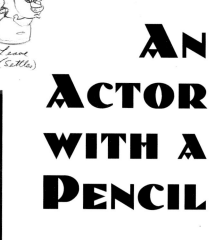

Small planning drawings or "thumbnails" of Hugo spitting feathers (above). Quasimodo sings the emotional last line of "Out There" (top). Walks are difficult to animate (below right) because animators must consider weight, balance, rhythm, attitude, body language and, in this case, Mickey's dialogue as he goes in search of a giant, "I'll be seein' ya . . . I hope."

Imagine that you are a famous actor who has just been hired to appear in a big Hollywood movie. Like any good actor, you read the script, study your lines, and do wardrobe and hair tests. On your first day of shooting you arrive on the movie set, but just as the cameras are about to roll, the director steps up to you and says, "Here's a pencil. Why don't you draw your performance instead?" That's what an **ANIMATOR** does every day. ■ Animators really are actors who draw. Just like a director casting a live-action role, the directors of an animated film must decide which animator will be best to work on each particular character. That's because individual animators, like actors, have individual strengths and weaknesses. One may be great with comedy, another with dialogue scenes, another with action. ■ But unlike actors in most live-action films, an animator can crawl into the skin of a wide variety of characters. Andreas Deja animated Gaston, Jafar, Scar, and then Mickey Mouse. James Baxter animated Roger Rabbit, then Belle, then Rafiki, then Quasimodo. ■ With all of the research complete, the

AN ACTOR WITH A PENCIL

animator and directors meet to discuss the character's action, motivation, mood, gestures, and so on. They'll listen together to the voice performance and look at the character's movements in the story reel. ■ Then the directors and animator focus on

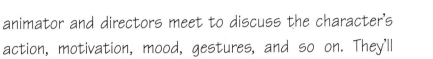

A TYPICAL ANIMATED FILM HAS ABOUT 1,300 INDIVIDUAL SCENES OR CUTS IN IT.

one scene to actually begin animation. It is at this "issuing session" that the animator gets the layout drawing and all the materials for the scene he or she is about to animate. A typical animated film has about 1,300 individual scenes or cuts in it. Each scene is issued to

an animator and discussed at length with the directors before work begins. Often the directors and animator will act out the action in the scene for one another so the assignment is clear. ■ Then the animator draws thumbnails, which are small sketches of the action in the scene. The animator will show these thumbnail sketches to the directors and, after more discussion, the work begins.

Animators know that most living creatures move in very fluid circular paths called arcs. The arc of Pocahontas's dive makes it seem very natural (above).

Sometimes animators use a mirror to study facial expressions and mouth shapes (left) and a stopwatch to time the length of an action while acting it out (opposite).

Rough animation drawings can be packed with passion and power, like this drawing of the Beast (left), or can make you laugh, like the drawing of Timon saying "luau" (opposite) or of Smee (bottom). Even a character without a face can be an actor, as these sketches of The Flying Carpet from Aladdin show (above and opposite).

SNIFF SNIFF

DRAWINGS THAT LIVE

BOO HOO ...

Eric Larson summed up the unique quality of Disney animation with just one word—"sincerity." Putting a real, sincere, living performance on the screen using only drawings is no easy task. ■ When you go to see a movie,

NYA, NYA, NYA!

what you are really seeing is a piece of film traveling through a projector at a rate of twenty-four individual frames per second. So in simple terms, an animator must draw twenty-four drawings for every second of film. ■ Animators start by drawing the most extreme movements

of the scene. In the scene of Smee below, the animator drew these extremes:

**SMEE FLYING IN
LANDING
RECOVERING
LOOKS UP, SEES JUG
STRETCHES TO CATCH IT
CATCHES THE JUG
RECOVERS**

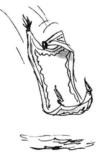

SPLASH

These seven extreme drawings are the basis of the animation. Between each of these extremes, the animator will want to do other drawings that break down the action even more. These drawings are called "breakdowns." ■ If this scene lasts five seconds on the screen, the animator may do only two or three dozen of the 120 drawings (5 seconds X 24 drawings per second) needed for that scene. The animator's assistant will do a portion of the

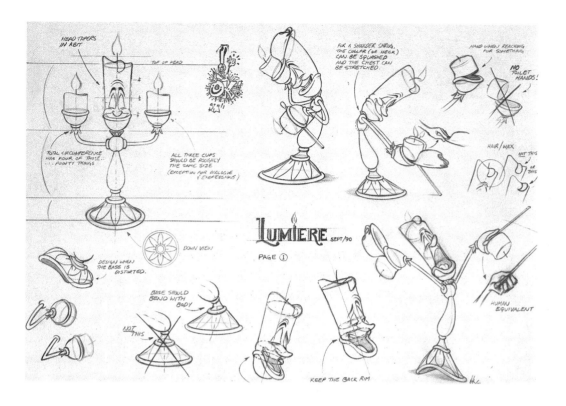

These study notes of Tigger from animator Walt Stanchfield (below) show the dozens of things an animator must be aware of when drawing. The supervising animator makes up a model sheet filled with drawings and notes (right) so everyone in his or her unit will draw the character in the same way.

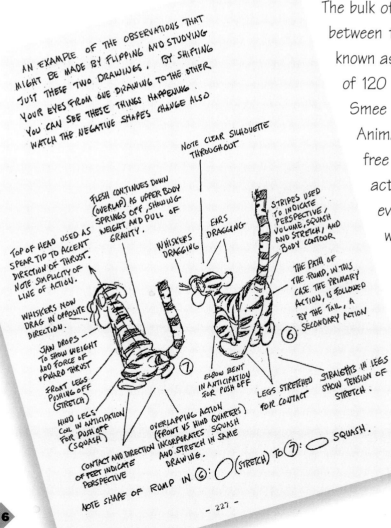

remaining drawings, but only the most important ones. The bulk of the remaining drawings—those that fall in between the finished drawings—are done by artists known as **INBETWEENERS**. The result is a stack of 120 drawings that, if flipped in sequence, have Smee come to life and make a diving catch. ■

Animators work with rough drawings that are very free and expressive. The drawing must portray action, mood, timing, weight, and volume. And every drawing must look like the character—what the animators call being "on model." The animator works holding a pencil in one hand and the sheets of paper in the other hand, one sheet between each finger. Animation paper has holes punched in the bottom so it can be put on pegs. The pegs keep the drawings in order and allow the animator to flip quickly between the drawings. This flipping lets the animator see how the drawings relate to one another.

The round animator's "disc" (above) lets the artist spin the drawing around to reach difficult angles. The center of the disc is glass with lights below so the artist can see through several layers of paper. Punched animation paper fits on pegs to allow the animator to draw with one hand and flip back and forth between drawings with the other hand to see the movement.

Animators always look for something appealing in a drawing. What could be more appealing than this Bill Tytla drawing from Dumbo (right).

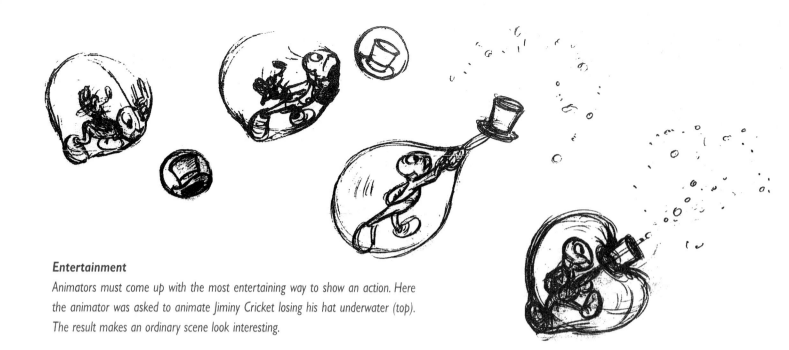

Entertainment

Animators must come up with the most entertaining way to show an action. Here the animator was asked to animate Jiminy Cricket losing his hat underwater (top). The result makes an ordinary scene look interesting.

Silhouette

Can you understand what's happening in this drawing (left) even when the character is blackened in? This principle, which animators call "silhouette," is a good test to see if the animation drawing is communicating or "reading" clearly to the audience.

Flipping

Animators "flip" a stack of animation drawings to see the movement (below).

Squash and Stretch

Animators can make a drawing look more alive by squashing and stretching the shapes. Move your eyes back and forth between the drawings below to observe how Edgar's mouth and double chin alternately squash and stretch.

Dialogue

To make a character "talk," the dialogue is recorded first. Then an editor listens to the recorded dialogue and gives the animator a very detailed breakdown of all the vowel and consonant sounds. This breakdown, called a "sound reading," is entered on a document called an "exposure sheet" (right). See if you can find the sound reading for "My hat! My umbrella!" Each horizontal line on the exposure sheet represents one frame of film, so the animator knows how many frames it takes to say a word. Now the animator can make drawings for each vowel and consonant sound. When played with the sound track, these drawings of Edgar (bottom) will appear to say, "My hat! My umbrella!"

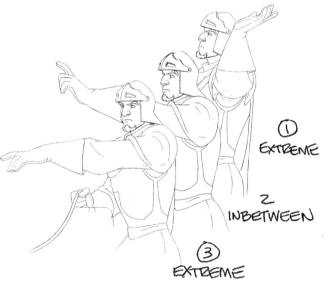

① EXTREME

2 INBETWEEN

③ EXTREME

TIMING CHART

① 2 ③

Inbetweens

Inbetweens are the drawings that come between an animator's extreme drawings. A timing chart (above) tells the inbetweener where to space his or her drawings to complete an action. Here the animator wants the inbetween (drawing two) to favor drawing three. Notice how the spacing of Phoebus's hand reflects the spacing on the timing chart.

Clean Me Up

The next step is for the stack of animation drawings to be shot on videotape. This lets the animators and directors look at the animation to see if the acting is working. Just as everyone's handwriting is slightly different, every animator's drawing style is different, too. Each animator has his or her own personal style and draws a character in a different way. Some draw very loose, expressive drawings, others more precise drawings. ■ The character Quasimodo, for instance, was drawn by as many as eight different animators, each with a slightly different individual style. That's why there's a group of people called **CLEANUP ARTISTS** whose job it is to take the animation drawings and redraw them with the essence of the animator's action and movement, while at the same time making it look as though the character—and in fact the whole movie—was drawn by one person. ■ The cleanup artist starts with the animator's extreme drawings. A fresh piece of paper is put over the animator's rough drawing and the artist makes a new, cleaned-up drawing. The animator checks the drawings to ensure the animation is still working. Then these cleaned-up drawings, called keys, are in betweened to create the twenty-four final drawings needed for every second of film. ■ Cleanup is a detail-oriented job. Buttons, teeth, tongues, and bits of overlapping action—like tails on lions, or hair on Pocahontas—are sometimes left off by the animators, who rely on the cleanup artists to supply all these details before a scene is put into color.

Cleanup artists use a size comparison sheet (top) to check the size relationships among characters. Animation drawings are studies of the forces of motion. They are often loose, quick drawings with little detail (opposite top and lower left). The cleanup artist must pin down the details, like hair and fur, that give the illusion of three-dimensional solidity. Imagine keeping track of all the spots on 101 Dalmatians or the stripes on Shere Khan (lower left). It takes patience, draftsmanship, and nerves of steel to be a cleanup artist (above). After all, the cleanup artist's drawings are the ones that actually appear on the screen (opposite right and below right).

THROUGH RAIN, SLEET, AND SNOW

Our story may be about people and places, but add the forces of nature and now you've got something. Wind, rain, sunlight, mist, fog, shadows, fire—all the domain of the **SPECIAL EFFECTS ANIMATOR**—help create a believable world and set the mood for the story. ■ Special effects artists are unique people. They are fascinated by the world of natural phenomena around us and are likely to enjoy drawing water splashes and bolts of lightning more than bunnies and bears. ■ When the character animators and cleanup artists are finished with their work, the special effects animator adds the shadows, props, and forces of nature in the scene. Literally everything that moves, other than the character, is added by the special effects animator. The technique is the same as in character animation—draw the extremes of the action first, then follow up with inbetweens to

Beneath Simba flames move from left to right as a visual reminder of the wildebeest stampede that rushed beneath Mufasa earlier in The Lion King. *The forces of nature swirl above the Sultan's palace (inset).*

break the animation down into twenty-four frames per second. ■ Computer workstations are also a tool to help the effects animator create rain showers, blowing snow, or glowing cinders from a fire. Computers also aid the effects artists in moving complex objects like Notre Dame's bells or Pocahontas's canoe. ■ As an experiment, study a sequence from a film like *The Lion King* and try to name all the bits of work that the special effects animator has done. The average audience may not think about it, but they sure would miss it if a character didn't have a shadow. Now it's time for the scene to move into the final production process.

Special effects supervisor Chris Jenkins studies real fire as he sketches Esmeralda in the flames (his drawings at right).

STYLIZED DEER LEAP FROM A WATERFALL WITH POCAHONTAS AND JOHN SMITH.

AN ANIMATED OCEAN CHURNS WHEN MONSTRO THE WHALE TURNS A CORNER.

WITH THE WAVE OF A MAGIC WAND, FAIRY DUST TURNS CINDERELLA INTO A PRINCESS.

FROLLO'S FIERY VISION OF ESMERALDA.

POCAHONTAS

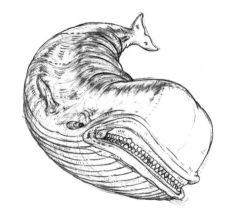

PINOCCHIO

CINDERELLA

It All Started with a Mouse

So far we've heard about artists who work with pencils, paper, paint, and brushes. But some of the artists on an animated film work on a computer with a keyboard and a mouse. ■ It's always funny when people say, "Wow, what computers can't do." That's like saying, "Wow, what pianos can't do" or "What baseball bats can't do." By themselves, pianos, baseball bats, and even computers can't do much. But give them to Elton John, Mickey Mantle, or a good animator, and they can create magic. Computers help the animation process in three ways:

CGI Computer Generated Imagery means just that—images on the screen that are animated with the help of a computer. Aladdin's flying carpet, a herd of thundering wildebeests, and a crowd of cheering people are all visual images that would take months and months to animate with pencil on a piece of paper. Computers make repetitive tasks fairly easy, so you can understand why the directors of *The Hunchback of Notre Dame* turned

> **CONSIDER MAKING EIGHT HUNDRED TOWNSPEOPLE MOVE AT TWENTY-FOUR FRAMES A SECOND FOR A SEQUENCE THAT LASTS SEVEN MINUTES—IMPOSSIBLE!**

to their **CGI ANIMATORS** to create thousands of cheering townspeople in the streets of Paris. A traditional animator might take an hour to draw a couple of townspeople. After a week the animator may have created a couple hundred drawings. Now consider making eight hundred townspeople move at twenty-four frames a second for a sequence like Topsy-Turvy that lasts seven minutes—impossible! As it is, the CGI animators took more than two years to create the crowds of Paris, even with the help of the computer.

CAPS Computer Animation Production System, an Academy Award–winning system, takes the cleaned-up animation drawings, colors them, combines them with the painted background, and then puts it all onto film to

form the final scene that you see in the theater. CAPS can also do millions of special effects, camera moves, and magic tricks that add to the look of a film—all of course with the aid of some very talented artists and technicians.

FAME Production managers, assistant production managers, and production auditors track the progress of the film with the aid of a computer program called FAME (Feature Animation Management Enhancer). FAME keeps careful track of the drawings, scenes, artists, and money that go into the making of an animated film.

Pages 66–67: Quasimodo swings down into the town square filled with hundreds of cheering computer-generated Parisians.

Artists can use CAPS to create endless effects, including this illusion of focus changing from the ants to the zebras (above). During the production of the wildebeest stampede (right) individual animals were tagged with fluorescent colors to make them easier to follow. CAPS combines CGI wildebeests with hand-drawn animation, the background, and computer-generated turbulence that looks like dust to create the final product (bottom and opposite).

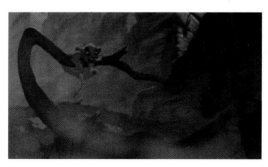

PUTTING IT TOGETHER

The final path to the screen is a complex one. Remember that an animated movie consists of about 1,300 individual "scenes." Each scene has now been storyboarded, laid out, recorded, issued by the director to an animator, animated, cleaned up, and finished off with the addition of visual effects. ■ The result of all this work is several stacks of animation drawings and a painted background. A document called an exposure sheet (x-sheet for short) is used to keep track of these stacks of drawings and exactly how they are to be combined. These drawings and paintings, created by the hands of dozens of artists, are scanned into the CAPS computer and combined (or composited) together, using the x-sheet as a road map, to create the final frame. ■ An amazing jack-of-all-trades artist called the **ARTISTIC COORDINATOR** plans and troubleshoots all of the artistic and technical aspects of the process. Randy Fullmer, artistic coordinator on *The Lion King*, describes it as "two trains (art and technology) colliding at high speed. My job is to end up with one big beautiful sleek train and not a train wreck."

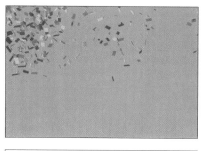

The original story sketch from Topsy-Turvy (opposite top left) inspired this scene that is made up of more than a dozen separate components. Artists use CAPS to combine all of these elements (above, left, and opposite) into the final shot (top). Color models (inset and near left) provide the painters with instructions on how to paint the characters.

SCANNING In scanning all the animation drawings and background paintings, done by hand, are scanned into the CAPS computer one at a time by a digital camera.

ANIMATION CHECK

Animation checkers ensure that all the drawings and details are present for a scene to be put into color. This is a really critical quality control point: It is here that the drawings, background paintings, CGI elements, and scene-planning information are carefully inspected in preparation for the final color operation.

SCENE PLANNING

Scene planning takes a creative idea and translates it into the technical language needed to bring that idea to the screen. For example, a layout artist or effects animator can meet with a scene planner and describe a desired effect. The planner then comes up with the technical solution to achieve that effect on the screen. Scene planners are terrific problem solvers and know the CAPS system like the backs of their hands.

COLOR MODEL

In color model, the colors for the characters and effects in each individual scene are selected. The art director and artistic coordinator stand in front of a color monitor like oil painters working on a canvas. With the color model artist, they tweak and play with the look of a scene like any painter would, but instead of paint and brush, they use electronic tools with funny-sounding names—blurs, ramps, tints, opacities, scale. They make minor adjustments to the colors and lighting of backgrounds, effects, and characters until the scene is a work of art.

SWEATBOX

This odd term is used to describe a meeting with the directors and department heads to critique individual scenes in the film. (It's named after Walt Disney's Moviola room, which was under a stairway and didn't have air-conditioning.) Here the directors look at the animation drawings that have been shot on black-and-white film—called pencil tests—and catch any mistakes in the character, effects, layout, or camera movement before a scene is put into color. If the scene looks good, the director will issue a "sweatbox note" and okay it to move on to the next step.

MARKUP

The information from animation check and color model is used to prepare the scene for inking and painting. This involves setting up palettes in the computer for each character or element in the scene as well as marking specific areas on each drawing so that the painters will know what to paint.

COMPOSITING

Combining all of the elements of a scene—painted background, painted characters, special effects, and computer elements—in their proper positions for each frame of the scene is called compositing. The composited scene is played back, checked, adjusted, and finally filmed.

FINAL CHECKING

Final check reviews a scene after it has been painted and composited. This is the first chance to preview what the scene will look like at full speed. All of the painting errors and anything else that isn't working can be fixed at this point.

INK AND PAINT

Many years ago, animation drawings were traced or photocopied onto a clear piece of celluloid (called a cel), and then painted on the reverse side with colorful paints. Today, with the CAPS computer, the character and effects drawings are inked and painted electronically, using a digital paint program and the palette of computer colors chosen by the color model staff.

FILM PRINTING

Each frame of the final scene has now been completed and composited at a very high resolution. The scene is photographed one frame at a time off of a cathode-ray tube onto thirty-five millimeter motion picture film. The film is processed, color balanced, and given to the editor to cut into the story reel.

Technology is rapidly changing in the editing suite. Here a computer helps the editor make quick changes to the picture and sound tracks in a filmless digital format.

Pages 74–75: The opening scene from Beauty and the Beast *and a rough animation drawing of Mickey Mouse.*

The picture and corresponding sound tracks can be played for viewing on a machine called a KEM.

A splicer and a roll of tape with filmlike perforations are used to cut and join pieces of film. Most feature films are made using 35-millimeter film (called that because it's 35 millimeters wide).

A Little off the Top, Please

An **EDITOR** is like a barber or a tailor, cutting and trimming the film until it flows smoothly from one idea to the next. As one of the first people on the project, and one of the last ones off, the editor is a valuable creative collaborator for the directors. ■ On *The Hunchback of Notre Dame*, editor Ellen Keneshea cut together the recorded dialogue and story sketches to form the story reel. She assembled many different versions of the story reel in the early days of production; each version had a slightly different pace or content. The editor is always looking for the best ways to move the story along and keep the pace lively and interesting. ■ Once past this early stage, the process of upgrading the reels with bits of completed animation and color begins. The editor is constantly making fine trims, nips, and tucks so the pacing of the film will feel natural to the viewer. Along the way, assistant editors help keep track of the thousands of feet of film and hundreds of sound recordings. ■ Toward the end of production, the editor works with the **SOUND EFFECTS EDITORS** and **MUSIC EDITORS** to support the story with sound. The editor also works with the film lab at the very end of the project as the prints of the film are color balanced and quality checked prior to release.

Editors use a synchronizer (above) to make sure the picture and sound elements work together in sync. Here the picture and three tracks of sound—for dialogue, music, and sound effects—run through the synchronizer. The sound track is made of clear 35-millimeter film coated with magnetic recording material (the same material used for audiocassette tapes).

The final film you see at the movies has the picture on the right and a tiny sound track, called an optical track, on the left. The sound is created when a beam of light passes through the "squiggles" on the optical track.

MAKE MINE MUSIC

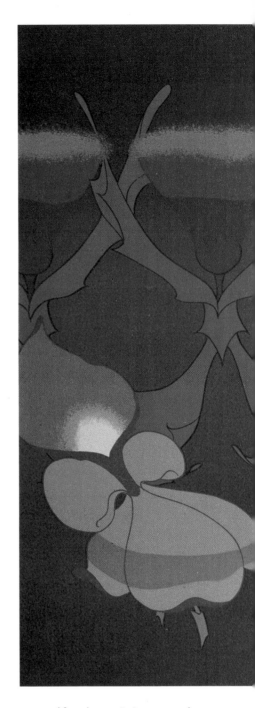

In animation, music and art are inseparable. No animated film illustrates this better than *Fantasia*, which combines music and animation (without a word of dialogue) for an amazing result. ■ The music in a film, or score (the last layer of storytelling applied to the film), can be in beautiful harmony with the art on the screen. The scoring is different from the songs discussed earlier: Songs—"Hakuna Matata," "Be Our Guest"—come and go, but the scoring music runs nearly the entire length of the film and emphasizes the emotions on the screen. ■ A few months before the movie is completed, the composer looks at the film with the directors and discusses the feeling of the story—then he or she turns those ideas into music. A full orchestra of musicians is assembled to record the score. The conductor directs the orchestra while watching the movie on a video monitor so that the music will be performed in sync with the action on the screen. ■ Some movie scores call for special sounds. Hans Zimmer traveled to Africa to record Zulu singers chanting over the sound track of *The Lion King*. Alan Menken went to a cathedral to record the church choirs and pipe organs that give *The Hunchback of Notre Dame* its celestial sound. ■ Alan wrote not only the songs for *The Little Mermaid*, *Beauty and the Beast*, *Aladdin*, *Pocahontas*, and *The Hunchback of Notre Dame* but the scores, too. He takes melodic elements from the songs and incorporates them in the score. Not only do you hear Quasimodo sing "Out There" early in the movie, but you hear the song again and again in the score each time you see him venture out into the world.

After the music is composed, an orchestrator works with the film composer to spread the music out over a seventy-piece symphony orchestra (shown opposite left, recording the score of The Hunchback of Notre Dame). The conductor uses a master score with the musicians' parts written on it (opposite right) and conducts while watching the film so that the music fits the action on the screen.

Sounds Like Fun

Stop for a minute and listen to all the sounds going on around you right now. Do you hear cars? An air conditioner or refrigerator running? A clock ticking? Crickets? We don't often think about it, but our world is full of sounds. Sound effects help create a more realistic world on the screen. ■ Here's a little experiment. What would happen if you had to close your eyes and figure out where you were just by what you heard? List what you would hear if you were in the following places:

DOWNTOWN NEW YORK CITY

A SKI SLOPE IN COLORADO

A PET STORE

A COLONY ON THE MOON

PARIS IN 1487

A BASEBALL STADIUM

A FARM IN THE EARLY MORNING

A SEASIDE VILLAGE

AT THE DINNER TABLE WITH A FAMILY

Your list probably contains a lot of general sounds called backgrounds. These background sounds help an animated film seem more real and three-dimensional. Some sounds—like the sound the Beast's magic mirror makes—are designed specifically for a film. Other, more general sounds like rooster crows or car horns can be found

What sounds would you give to this scene of Scar?

in a sound effects library. ■ Another way to make sounds is to use the Foley process, which is named after the man who invented it. In the Foley process, the movie is projected on a video screen while the sound effects artist makes sounds that match the picture. Footsteps, movement of cloth or paper, and any other sounds that have to synchronize closely with the picture are recorded this way. ■ All of the audio elements of a movie are taken to a place called a mixing stage for a process called the final dub. Dubbing is the process of combining dialogue, sound effects, and music to form the final sound track for the film. ■ Three people called mixers (one each for dialogue, music, and sound effects) preside over a huge mixing panel with volume controls for each individual element of sound. It's a very detailed job because each footstep, inhale, gust of wind, or twig snap is isolated on its own track so the mixers can manipulate the volume and quality of that sound in the mix. The directors and mixers look at the picture and listen to each moment in the film over and over to try to arrive at the right combination of dialogue, music, and sound effects to best tell the story. Sometimes the dialogue is the most important thing in a scene and the music is played softly or not at all. In other sequences, music is everything. ■ Terry Porter, who has supervised the mix on most of Disney's recent animated films, says it's like being a chef—"mixing together the sound ingredients until it tastes just right."

Years before multitrack recording was invented, voices, music, and sound effects had to be recorded at the same time (right). Now each sound is recorded and controlled separately, using a sophisticated mixing panel (background). At the movie theater, sound comes from three speakers behind the screen and surround speakers on the sides of the theater.

The Hunchback of Notre Dame
Production 1483

DRAFT

Printed: Thu 08/03/95 15:59

	Footage	Description Of Action
T THERE Trousdale/Wise 403 - 03		
Artist LO: ST PIERRE A: BAXTER BG: ALTIERI CU LO: SHANNON	12 - 13	CU Toy Village. Quasi's hand enters and picks up Quasi doll. [O.S.] Frollo: "OUT THERE THEY'LL REVILE YOU AS A MONSTER." DIAGONAL PAN TO MCU as Quasi brings the doll up to his face. Quasi: "I AM A MONSTER" Quasi picks up another doll and looks at them both. [O.S.] Frollo: "OUT THERE THEY WILL HATE AND SCORN AND JEER." Quasi "ONLY A MONSTER."
9.00 LO: GHERTNER A: ZIELINSKI BG: STIMPSON CU LO: CAPLE	6 - 03	MED. CU Frollo (UPSHOT). Frollo: "WHY INVITE THEIR CALUMNY AND CONSTERNATION?"
910.00 LO: MARTIN A: COSTA PUDLEINER BG: LORENCZ CU LO: WEINHART	2 - 15	MED TWO SHOT as Frollo blocks Quasi from playing with his toys. The TABLE and CATHEDRAL are in the FOREGROUND. Frollo lowers his arm toward the table. Frollo: "STAY IN HERE." CU Quasi's POV as Frollo's arm and hand sweep the toys off the table.
0011.00 LO: GHERTNER A: PUDLEINER BG: LORENCZ CU LO: CRAIG JR	8 - 10	[O.S.] Frollo: "BE FAITHFUL TO ME." Quasi: "I'M FAITHFUL" Frollo sets a basket of food on the table. [O.S.] Frollo: "GRATEFUL TO ME" Quasi: "I'M GRATEFUL" MCU Quasi as he holds up the Quasi doll. Frollo's hand enters from the left and takes the doll from
03.0/012.00 LO: ST PIERRE A: COSTA BG: ALTIERI CU LO: SHANNON	6 - 13	Quasi. DIAGONAL PAN UP following Frollo's hand. [O.S.] Frollo: "DO AS I SAY. OBEY." MED TWO SHOT. Frollo places the Quasi doll back in the balcony of the belltower.
03.0/013.00 LO: MARTIN A: YOUNG ZIELINSKI BG: LORENCZ CU LO: GHERTNER	9 - 15	Frollo: "AND STAY IN HERE." Quasi: "I'LL STAY IN HERE" MCU Quasi looking up at [O.S]. Frollo. Frollo's shadow crosses over his face. Quasi: "YOU ARE GOOD TO ME, MASTER."
03.0/014.00 LO: ST PIERRE A: YOUNG BG: ALTIERI CU LO: SHANNON	5 - 14	Quasi turns his head screen right following [O.S.] Frollo leaving. Quasi: "I AM SORRY." FS Frollo. His back is to the camera as he walks away. Frollo: "YOU ARE FORGIVEN."
03.0/015.00 LO: BIELICKI A: ZIELINSKI BG: STIMPSON CU LO: WILSON	2 - 08	

Page: 22

Copyright 1995 Walt Disney Pictures

An animation studio is a busy place, especially during the final months of production. A draft (above) is a document that describes each scene in the film and other details.

GETTING IT ON THE SCREEN

At times, the chaos and complexity of making an animated movie can seem like a three-ring circus. As with any circus, there is a ring-master who keeps things in order and moving along. In animation, the ringmasters are the production people. ■ Way back in the beginning of this book, we talked about the head ringmaster—the producer. The producer is the team builder, cheerleader, creative partner, and the buck-stops-here person. The producer's job, though, can be summed up in just one word—"quality." The quality of all the work that goes into an animated movie will still be remembered long after the budget and schedule are forgotten. ■ The **ASSOCIATE PRODUCER** has three things (three *big* things) to worry about—people, time, and money. Associate producers are always solving problems that sound like they come from some nightmarish math test. For example: If four animators can each animate three seconds of film each week and an assistant can clean up two seconds of film each week and there are twenty weeks left to finish the film, how many assistants will you need each week to finish cleanup on time? You might say that the answer is six assistants, but the real answer is "We never finish cleanup on time." The art of producing and managing an animated movie has to allow for changes and false starts and animation that doesn't always work the first time around. Remember quality?

The **PRODUCTION MANAGER** looks at the work to be done and the creative needs of all the artists, and then schedules the directors' time so they're in the right place at the right time—so everyone can make the most effective use of their time. It's no small task. Being a production manager for an animated film is like being the mayor of a small city. ■ Each department of an animated production runs like its own little business. A department head and an assistant production manager (APM for short) run the business. The department head is an artist who ensures that the quality of the product (be it backgrounds or effects scenes) is the best it can be. The APM manages weekly schedules and people to make sure that, little by little, the department is doing its part to complete the film on time. ■ Then there are armies of tireless production secretaries, production assistants, and coordinators, who do everything from typing scripts and memos to arranging for catering during the production crunch, answering phones, running errands, and generally helping move the production ahead. ■ Creativity doesn't just happen on the drawing board. Imagine producing an eighty-minute movie—you have to manage twenty-five layout artists, fifty animators, 120 assistants and inbetweeners, twenty-three special effects artists, eighteen background painters, four computer animators, as well as checkers, scene planners, painters, and assorted other artists and technicians, totaling about six hundred people over a four-year period. Now that takes creativity!

Production reports (above right) help the production staff keep track of each department's progress. Good communication is essential in production, and phone calls are constant.

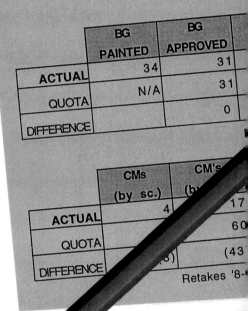

THE HUNCHBACK
Weekly Totals
W/E 9/2/95

	RUFF LAYOUTS	INTO ANIMATION	ANI...
ACTUAL	43	179	
QUOTA	32	145	
DIFFERENCE	11	34	Part

	BG PAINTED	BG APPROVED
ACTUAL	34	31
QUOTA	N/A	31
DIFFERENCE		0

	CMs (by sc.)	CM's (b...	
ACTUAL	4		17
QUOTA			60
DIFFERENCE		(8)	(43)

Retakes '8-

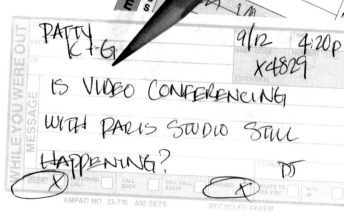

DATE 6/23 TIME 7:02
PHONE 6010 AREA CODE PHON
FAX AREA CODE PHON

DATE 10:00
AREA CODE TIME 8:30 (AM/PM)
NO 8624
2:00

PATTY
K+G
9/12 4:20p
X4829

IS VIDEO CONFERENCING WITH PARIS STUDIO STILL HAPPENING?
DT

URGENT X

POCAHONTAS OPENING IN CENTRAL PARK

A Night at the Movies

The opening of a Disney animated feature has become something of an event. The days leading up to the premiere screening are filled with last-minute adjustments and polishes. ■ A film is often previewed three or four times before it is completed, to find out what a real audience will think of it. People are recruited from shopping malls and street corners to come see the work in progress. If you were in the audience for a preview screening, you would be asked to fill out a questionnaire from the filmmakers, asking what your favorite and least favorite things about the movie were. After each preview, the filmmakers huddle to discuss the audience's comments and decide what little changes could be made to help refine the movie.

Questionnaires like this (right) help the filmmakers understand how a preview audience reacted to the film. One hundred thousand people jam New York City's Central Park (opposite left) for the opening of Pocahontas. *Tickets to the premiere of* The Lion King *(opposite right) and the final scene of* The Rescuers Down Under *(background).*

1. What would you tell your friends about The Lion King? (MARK AN "X" IN THE BOX THAT DESCRIBES HOW YOU FEEL) (06(

It was GREAT ☒ 1

It was VERY GOOD ☐ 2

It was GOOD ☐ 3

It was NOT GOOD ☐ 4

It was BAD ☐ 5

3. How would you describe the movie, The Lion
   It was reallygre
   ao and coo it

4. What did you like and what did you not like

   Things I Liked
   1. I liked Everything
   2. _____
   3. _____
   4. _____
   5. _____

5. Here are the songs which were in the movie. Pl
   liked most and the one song which was your favo

   Circle Of Life (opening song)..................
   Can't Wait To Be King (Young Simba's song)...(
   Be Prepared (Scar's song).....................(
   Hakuna Matata (Pumbaa and Timon's song).....(
   Can You Feel The Love Tonight (Simba and
   Nala's love song in the jungle)............(

6. What character did you like best in the movie?
   Simba's Dad

7. What character did you like least in the movie?
   Scar

8. How old are you? ___ 4

9. Are you a:

BOY

Then comes the moment of truth—opening night, when the lights go down and the finished movie is shared with the public for the first time. With a little luck, all the details I've described throughout this book combine to form a movie experience which, ironically, should make you forget you are looking at drawings at all. The audience response to animation, as with any art form, is an emotional one. Animation speaks to the heart. Regardless of language, it can inspire and entertain like no other medium.

Memorable moments from Pocahontas *(background),* The Lion King *(right), and* Beauty and the Beast *(below).*

How Can I Learn More?

Well, that's the end of your backstage journey for now. But the magic doesn't end here. There's so much more to learn about the animation process. If you dream of someday working at an animation studio, here are some tips from the pros:

■ Draw a little bit every day. Talent is important, but it takes lots of practice and hard work to be an animation artist.

■ Draw with a pencil. That's what animators use most of the time.

■ Draw from life. Copying cartoons doesn't do much good. Character animation is based on real people, animals, and things.

■ Take some art classes at your local accredited art school, junior college, or university. Most of these schools have good classes in the fundamentals of art.

■ Tell your art teacher you are interested in becoming an animator.

■ Look for books on drawing and animation at your library or bookstore (see the bibliography in this book for some ideas).

Disney artists take classes, visit zoos, look at books and films, attend lectures, draw, paint, think, and write notes. You can do the same thing. You might even pretend that you are making your own animated movie. Here's an idea that might help you get started. First pick a topic you like—hockey, for example. How would you write a story about two hockey teams that were getting ready for a championship game? Then try drawing hockey players. Are the players kids or adults? Humans or animals? Is one team the nasty favorite and the other the heroic underdog? What color would you pick for the underdog team's jersey and what color for the opponent? Would the big game be played

Animators' quick sketches and studies of real people and animals (opposite). Goofy on ice (below) from the cartoon Hockey Homicide. An animator used a computer instead of a pencil to animate Buzz Lightyear in Toy Story (above).

at noon on a frozen lake or at night in a sports arena? Would the teams have mascots? A coach? A funny goalie? A stupid referee? You get the idea. ■ And if you're not an artist but a fan, let this book be the beginning of your exploration into the magic of animation. Books like *The Art of The Lion King*, *The Art of Pocahontas*, or *The Art of The Hunchback of Notre Dame* provide detailed insight into the making of these special films. There are other kinds of animation to explore, too. Look at the stop-motion animation in films like *The Nightmare Before Christmas* or the groundbreaking computer-animated film *Toy Story*. They are produced with completely different techniques that will make your head spin. ■ The dictionary defines animation this way: "to impart life to; to inspire with energy or action; to enliven." I still define it in the same way I did when I was a kid . . .

it's Magic!

GLOSSARY OF TERMS

Animac—Trade name for a computer program that allows the animator to scan in his/her drawings and then adjust the rate at which the drawings play back on the screen. This tool helps the animator adjust the timing of the action in the scene.

Animation paper—Rectangular drawing paper with holes punched in the bottom to keep individual animation drawings in registration with one another.

Animator—An artist/actor who creates a series of drawings that, when viewed in rapid succession, appear to come to life.

APM—Assistant Production Manager. Manages various departments in animation and reports to the production manager.

Art director—An artist who is responsible for the visual look and design of the entire movie.

Artistic coordinator—A trouble-shooter/artist who deals with artistic and technical problems.

Aspect ratio—The ratio of screen height to screen width. Most movies have a 1 to 1.85 aspect ratio. Some wide-screen movies like *Sleeping Beauty* have a 1 to 2.35 aspect ratio.

Associate producer—The person who deals with production issues like people, time, money, etc.

Background—The painting that appears behind the animated characters.

Blue sketch—After animation is done, a tracing that shows the path of action of animated characters. Used by layout and background artists so they can plan props and lighting that won't interfere with the characters' movement.

Breakdown—An intermediate drawing between the animator's key drawings.

CAPS—Computer Animation Production System. Disney's Academy Award–winning system that helps the artists assemble the animation, background, special effects, and computer-animated elements onto the final piece of film.

Casting—The process of finding the right person to play a role.

CGI—Computer Generated Imagery. Elements of the film that are created by computer animators and technicians— e.g., the Beast's ballroom, the wildebeest stampede, and Aladdin's magic carpet.

Checking—The process of looking at all the drawings, paintings, and camera movements in an individual scene to ensure that everything is properly done before the scene moves on to the next production step. Scenes are checked twice—animation check when a scene is still pencil drawings and final check when a scene is in color and ready to go to film.

Cleanup—The art of refining an animator's rough, expressive drawings into the final, detailed drawings that will be scanned and painted to create the final color scene.

Color key—A small color sketch that illustrates what a particular sequence will look like in the final movie.

Color model—Part of the process where character colors are assigned. Also when characters, backgrounds, special effects, and computer graphics elements are all previewed together for the first time. The art director makes countless adjustments to get the scene to look just right.

Comparative size sheet—A drawing of each character side by side so that the artists can understand a character's height and size in relationship to other characters.

Composer—A musician who writes music for the film.

Compositing (or comping)— The act of assembling all the elements (character, background, effects) into each single frame of film at high resolution in preparation for film printing.

Contact shadow—A shadow that the character casts onto the ground or another object. Must be animated by an effects animator.

Credits (or screen credits)— The listing of the names of people who worked on the film.

Dailies—The daily shipment of film from the film lab. The directors look at this film, which is composed of shots in both color and black-and-white pencil.

Demo—An early rough version of a song, usually with just a piano or synthesizer and voice.

Development—The process of exploring an idea for a movie with writers and artists.

Digital film print—The process of transferring a scene from digital data on the CAPS system to motion picture film.

Director—The creative leader of a project. He or she coaches the actors, artists, and writers.

Dissolve (or cross-dissolve)— The effect of one scene fading out as the next scene fades in.

Draft—A document that describes in detail each individual scene in the movie, including the length of the scene (in feet and frames), the name of the animator, and a description of the action in the scene.

Dub (also called dubbing or mixing)— The process of combining sounds until the right balance of dialogue, music, and sound effects is achieved.

Editorial—A department responsible for all of the film and sound elements on a project. The supervising editor collaborates with the director to make sure the pacing of the film works.

Effects (or special effects)— Anything that moves but is not a character on the screen is called an effect. Effects animators create the drawings for these special effects in much the same way character animators create characters.

Effects editor (or sound effects editor)—The person who finds and places all of the sound effects needed to make the movie convincing.

Extreme—An animator's drawing that shows the extreme limits of an action. A scene of animation would be made up of several animators' extreme drawings.

FAME—A computer program that helps keep track of the progress of scenes in a film.

Field—What the camera sees.

Artwork must be drawn within the field for it to appear on-screen.

Flipping—Using the nondrawing hand to change quickly between drawings to see how the animation works.

Foley—A process of recording new sound effects while the film is being projected.

Footage—Film is measured in feet and frames, or footage. Sixteen frames equal 1 foot. There are ninety feet per minute of film. Footage often refers to the amount of footage a person or department created in a given week.

Frames—Motion picture film is made up of a string of individual pictures or frames that, when viewed in rapid succession, create the illusion of movement. There are twenty-four frames per second of film.

Inbetween—The drawings between the animator's key drawings. Artists who create these drawings are called inbetweeners.

Issuing—A meeting between animator and director during which a scene or group of scenes is discussed in detail and given to the animator to begin work.

KEM—A machine for viewing motion picture film with its corresponding sound tracks.

Key—An important drawing or painting that establishes the look of the surrounding artwork.

Layout—The pencil drawings of the set upon which the animated character will move.

Level—Artwork is sorted into different levels of drawings, i.e. the background level, the character level, the shadow level, the overlay level.

Live action—Motion picture photography of real people and things.

Maquette—A three-dimensional sculpture of a character.

Mix—Adjustment of individual sound elements to create a pleasing final combination of sounds.

Model sheet—A collection of drawings that illustrate how a character is drawn.

Multiplane—A camera setup with several levels of artwork that can move independently to create the illusion of depth. The CAPS computer creates similar effects.

Music editor—A person who makes sure the music written by the composer fits properly, or is in sync, with the picture. This person also keeps track of all musical elements on the film.

Optical track—The name for the sound track on the finished print of

the motion picture that runs in the theater.

Ones—If drawings are done for every frame of film, it's referred to as being "on ones."

Overlap—A character's appendages, such as long ears, skirts, or tails, that continue to move or "overlap": after the rest of the character has stopped.

Overlay—An additional drawing or painting on top of the layout or background that illustrates a foreground object.

Pan—The movement of a piece of artwork from side to side.

Pegs—The round or rectangular pegs that hold animation paper in order.

Pose—A drawing that shows a character in a particular attitude. Also refers to the animator's extreme drawings—e.g., "There are five poses in this scene."

Preview—A screening of the film for audience reaction, usually before the film is completed.

Producer—The person who supervises the making of the film.

Production auditor—The person who tracks time, productivity, and the expenditure of money.

Production manager—The person who coordinates work flowing through all departments on a production and manages the director's schedule.

Rims—The thin band of light on an edge of a character.

Rolling—The method of putting a drawing between each finger and rocking the drawings back and forth to see if the perceived motion is smooth.

Rotation—The tilting of the camera field.

Rough—A drawing that is done quickly and expressively to get an idea on paper.

Scanning—A process of photographing or, more correctly, digitizing a drawing into a computer so that it can be painted and combined with other drawings.

Scene—An individual cut in an animated film. Terminology in live-action filmmaking is different. There a sequence is a scene and a scene is called a shot or a cut.

Scene planning—The process of planning how the background, character, and effects will be combined and how the camera and artwork will move to create a sense of reality.

Script—The written document that describes the continuity and dialogue in a film.

Sequence—A chunk of storytelling usually centered around a particular location or piece of business, e.g., the ballroom sequence, the bell tower sequence, or the happy-ending sequence.

Sound reading—The editor's detailed breakdown of the vowel and consonant sounds in a line of dialogue, done prior to animating a scene.

Sound track—A recording of dialogue, music, or audible effects that is meant to accompany a motion picture.

Squash and stretch—A term to describe the constant tension and release of facial features or physical features on an animated character.

Stats (or photostats)—The frame-by-frame enlargements of live-action study film used for reference.

Story reel (or work reel)—A series of story sketches which have been shot in continuity on film and then edited together with dialogue to be viewed by the filmmakers.

Storyboard—The sequence of sketches pinned in consecutive order to tell a story.

Supervising animator—The animator in charge of a particular character in a movie.

Sweatbox—A meeting with the directors and key artists to critique individual scenes in the film. Named after Walt Disney's Moviola room, which was under a stairway and didn't have air-conditioning.

Sync (short for synchronous)—Elements of picture and sound being played together, at the same time.

Timing chart—An animator's note on a drawing to indicate to other artists how the inbetweens should be timed.

Tone mattes—Artwork created by an effects animator that gives a dark or shadowed side to a character.

Track—An individual sound element that runs in sync with the picture. There may be a separate track for dialogue, for music, and for sound effects. Also used in music recording with the same meaning—e.g., a trumpet track, a cello track, a percussion track.

Truck—The movement of the animation camera in and out.

Twos—In certain scenes of animation, an animator can do twelve drawings for every second of film instead of the usual twenty-four drawings. Each drawing is shot for two frames ("on twos") and the result still appears to be full animation.

Underscore—The movie music written to play under scenes of action or dialogue.

Workbook—A technical version of the storyboard with sketches that show how each scene will look in the final film.

X-sheet—Exposure sheet, the document that keeps track of all of the drawings and camera movements in an animation scene.

BIBLIOGRAPHY

OTHER BOOKS ABOUT ANIMATION YOU MAY FIND INTERESTING

Bendazzi, Giannalberto.
CARTOONS: ONE HUNDRED YEARS OF CINEMA ANIMATION.
Bloomington: University of Indiana Press, 1995.

Blair, Preston.
ANIMATION and **HOW TO ANIMATE FILM CARTOONS.**
New York: Walter T. Foster, 1980.

Jones, Chuck.
CHUCK AMUCK: THE LIFE AND TIMES OF AN ANIMATED CARTOONIST.
New York: Farrar, Straus & Giroux, 1989.

Laybourne, Kit.
THE ANIMATION BOOK: A COMPLETE GUIDE TO ANIMATED FILMMAKING FROM FLIP-BOOKS TO SOUND CARTOONS.
New York: Crown, 1979.

Maltin, Leonard.
OF MICE AND MAGIC: A HISTORY OF AMERICAN ANIMATED CARTOONS.
New York: McGraw-Hill, 1980.

Solomon, Charles.
THE HISTORY OF ANIMATION: ENCHANTED DRAWINGS.
New York: Wings Books, 1994.

Thomas, Bob.
DISNEY'S ART OF ANIMATION: FROM MICKEY MOUSE TO BEAUTY AND THE BEAST.
New York: Hyperion, 1991.

Thomas, Frank, and Ollie Johnston.
THE ILLUSION OF LIFE: DISNEY ANIMATION.
New York: Hyperion, 1995.

DON HAHN has produced some of the most critically acclaimed animated motion pictures of this generation, including *The Hunchback of Notre Dame*, *The Lion King*, and *Beauty and the Beast*, the first animated film ever nominated for an Academy Award for best picture. He was associate producer of *Who Framed Roger Rabbit*, the groundbreaking 1988 film that pioneered new techniques for combining animation and live action. Born in Chicago, Don Hahn began his career at Walt Disney Studios in 1976 as assistant director to veteran animation producer-director Wolfgang Reitherman.

THE DISNEY ANIMATION CREW (ABOVE) IN FRONT OF THEIR STUDIOS IN BURBANK, CALIFORNIA. BELOW IS A LISTING OF THE EXTRAORDINARY ARTISTS WHOSE WORK FILLS THE PAGES OF THIS BOOK.

Page 1 Lumiere by Debra Armstrong and Nik Ranieri.

Page 4/5 *The Hunchback of Notre Dame* background by Michael Humphries; Ugly Duckling, artist unknown.

Page 8/9 *The Hunchback of Notre Dame* painting by Rowland Wilson; *The Jungle Book* by Ken Anderson.

Page 10/11 Bambi by Tyrus Wong; Sorcerer by Joe Grant; *The Jungle Book* by Bill Peet; *The Hunchback of Notre Dame* by Vance Gerry; Basil and Olivia by Vance Gerry; *The Sword in the Stone* by Vance Gerry.

Page 12/13 Aladdin procession by Sue Nichols; *The Lion King* sketch by Vance Gerry.

Page 14/15 Cogsworth and Lumiere by Roger Allers and Hans Bacher; Pocahontas by Glen Keane; *The Lion King* by Chris Sanders.

Page 16/17 Beast transformation by Chris Sanders; wildebeest stampede by Thom Enriquez; Mufasa's ghost by Chris Sanders; Pumbaa and Timon by Barry Johnson.

Page 18/19 Aladdin and Jasmine by Glen Keane; Simba by Ruben Aquino; Laverne by Tony Fucile; Pocahontas and Meeko by Glen Keane and Nik Ranieri; Cruella De Vil by Marc Davis; Frollo by Kathy Zielinski.

Page 20/21 Ed by Alex Topete and Dave Burgess; Rafiki by James Baxter.

Page 24/25 Scar concept drawing by Andreas Deja.

Page 26 Shenzi and Banzai story sketches by Barry Johnson; Dopey by Fred Moore.

Page 28/29 *The Hunchback of Notre Dame* painting by Justin Brandstater; *The Lion King* by Don Moore; *The Hunchback of Notre Dame* by David Goetz; Pocahontas by Michael Giaimo.

Page 30/31 Aladdin palace by Richard Vander Wende; Aladdin layout explorations by Bill Perkins; *The Rescuers Down Under* pastel by Maurice Hunt; Aladdin notes and sketch by Richard Vander Wende; Aladdin painting by Kathy Altieri.

Page 32/33 *101 Dalmatians* by Walt Peregoy; Skull Rock by Ken O'Connor; Cinderella concept by Mary Blair; Quasimodo's table by Gil Hung; *Alice in Wonderland* concept by Mary Blair.

Page 34/35 Chernabog by Bill Tytla; Peter Pan painting by Claude Coats.

Page 36/37 Jasmine's room by Bill Perkins; Gaston's pub by Ed Ghertner; medieval Paris cleaned-up layout by Lam Hoang; riverbend by Karen Keller and Lissa Ainley from a concept by Rasoul Azadani.

Page 38/39 *The Lion King* workbook by Dan St. Pierre; *The Hunchback of Notre Dame* workbook by Sam Michlap; *The Lion King* workbook by Tom Shannon.

Page 40/41 Paris layout by Fred Craig.

Page 42/43 Aladdin color key by Richard Vander Wende; background from *Lady and the Tramp* by Claude Coats; *The Hunchback of Notre Dame* color keys by David Goetz and Lisa Keene.

Page 44/45 Pocahontas background by Allison Belliveau-Proulx; Pocahontas key by Sunny Apinchapong; Aladdin key by Richard Vander Wende; Sleeping Beauty key by Eyvind Earle; *The Hunchback of Notre Dame* keys by Lisa Keene and Colin Stimpson.

Page 46/47 Pinocchio by Claude Coats; *101 Dalmatians* by Walt Peregoy; *The Hunchback of Notre Dame* by Gregory Alexander Drolette; Bambi and Alice in Wonderland paintings, artist unknown.

Page 48/49 Mad Hatter by Ward Kimball; Pinocchio by Frank Thomas; Cinderella by Marc Davis; Mufasa by Tony Fucile; Esmeralda by Tony Fucile; Ursula by Rob Minkoff; *Lady and the Tramp* drawing, artist unknown; Pocahontas by Renee Holt-Bird and Glen Keane; Geppetto, artist unknown; Belle by Brian McEntee.

Page 50/51 Clopin sculpture by Kent Melton; warthog and lion sketches by Andreas Deja; mandrill drawings by Glen Keane; recording session sketches by Mark Henn; Native American by Michael Cedeno; Cruella De Vil and Anita by Marc Davis and Milt Kahl.

Page 52/53 Hugo thumbnails by Dave Pruiksma; Quasimodo by James Baxter; Russ Edmonds and Don Hahn (pictured); Pocahontas by Glen Keane; Mickey Mouse by Fred Moore; Michael Surrey (pictured).

Page 54/55 Beast by Glen Keane; Aladdin's carpet by Ed Gombert and Randy Cartwright; Smee by Ollie Johnson; Timon by Rob Minkoff.

Page 56/57 Tigger by Milt Kahl; Lumiere by Nik Ranieri; Dumbo by Bill Tytla; Ron Husband (pictured).

Page 58/59 Jiminy Cricket by Ward Kimball; Edgar by Milt Kahl; Roger (silhouette) by Milt Kahl; Phoebus by Brian Clift and Dave Brewster.

Page 60/61 Shere Khan by Stan Green and Milt Kahl; *The Hunchback of Notre Dame* comparative size chart by Vera Lanpher; Peg cleanup by George Goepper and rough drawing by Eric Larson; Pocahontas cleanup by Renee Holt-Bird and rough drawing by Glen Keane.

Page 64/65 Pocahontas stylized deer by Karen Keller; Pocahontas waterfall effects by Tom Hush; deer by GeeFwee Boedoe; Monstro by Woolie Reitherman; water by Josh Meador and Dan MacManus; Cinderella by Marc Davis; Esmeralda in flames by Chris Jenkins.

Page 70 Clopin story sketch by Kevin Harkey.

Page 74/75 Mickey, artist unknown.

Page 76 Pictured: Ellen Keneshea; Jacki Kinney (standing), John Carr, and Jessica Ambinder-Rojas.

Page 81 Pictured: orchestra conducted by Frank Churchill; Bill Garity is the engineer.

Page 88 Volleyball by James Fujii; stroller by Pres Romanillos; llama by Andreas Deja; café by Walt Stanchfield.

Page 89 Goofy on ice by Milt Kahl.

Page 94 Mrs. Potts by Brian McEntee.

Additional photography by Michael Ginsburg, Robert Isenberg, Michael Ansell, Richard Cartwright, and David Allocca.

ROBERT PUJDAK